◇TELL ME ABOUT◇

EVERYDAY THINGS

& HOW THEY WORK

SERIES EDITOR: JACKIE GAFF
ILLUSTRATED BY PETER BULL
& IAN MOORES

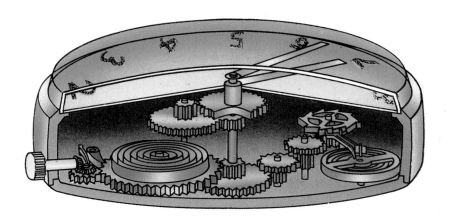

Kingfisher Books

Contents

Series editor: Jackie Gaff
Series designer: Terry Woodley

Author: Steve Parker
Contributor: Mary-Jane Wilkins
Designer: David West Children's Book Design
Illustrators: Peter Bull (pp. 4–10, 12, 14–17, 20–21,
26–27, 30–35); Ian Moores (pp. 2–3, 11, 13, 18–19,
22–25, 28–29, 36–38)
Cover illustration: Chris Forsey
Edited by: Veronica Pennycook

Kingfisher Books, Grisewood & Dempsey Ltd,
Elsley House, 24–30 Great Titchfield Street,
London W1P 7AD

First published in 1991 by Kingfisher Books
Copyright © Grisewood & Dempsey Ltd 1991

BRITISH LIBRARY CATALOGUING IN PUBLICATION DATA
Gaff, Jackie
Everyday things & how they work.
  I. Technology
  I. Title II. Bull, Peter III. Moores, Ian IV. Series
  600

ISBN 0 86272 562 3
All rights reserved.

Phototypeset by Southern Positives and Negatives
(SPAN), Lingfield, Surrey.
Printed in Spain.

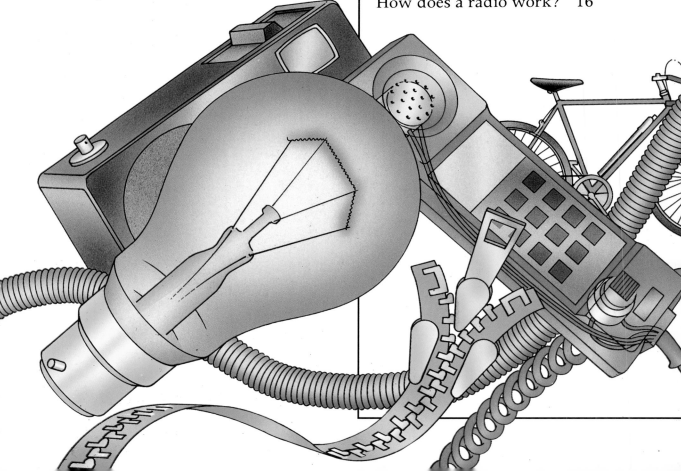

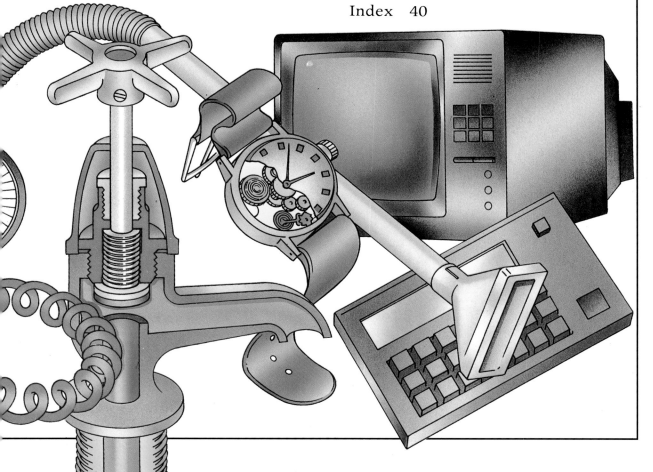

Where does electricity come from?

The electricity in a house comes from a power station. In all power stations, some kind of power pushes a huge wheel round very fast. This wheel turns an enormous machine called a generator, and it is this which makes the electricity. Some power stations get power from burning coal or oil. Others make electricity from the power of running water, or from nuclear power.

DON'T TOUCH

The electricity in the wall sockets of a house is powerful. Never poke things into the holes in a socket. It could kill you.

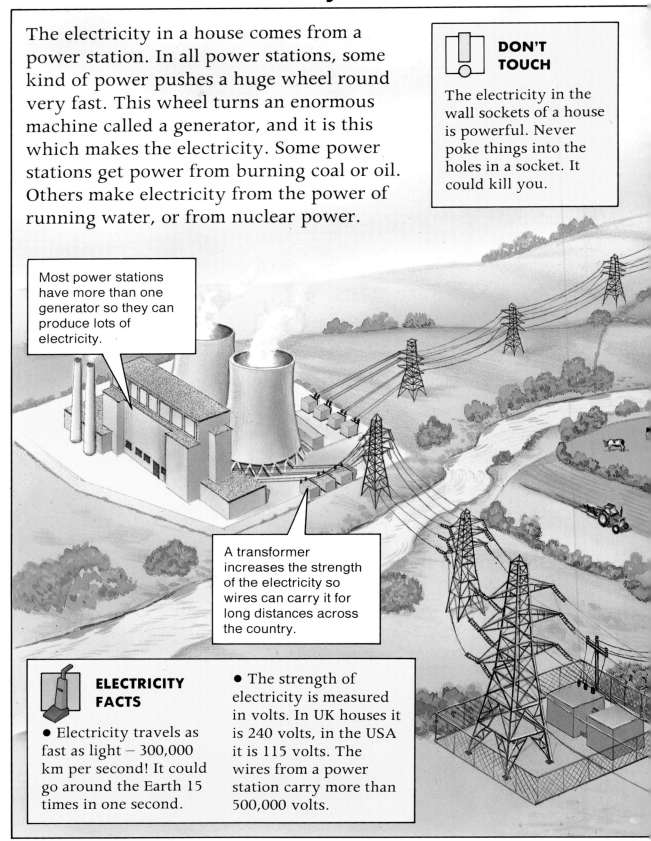

Most power stations have more than one generator so they can produce lots of electricity.

A transformer increases the strength of the electricity so wires can carry it for long distances across the country.

ELECTRICITY FACTS

● Electricity travels as fast as light – 300,000 km per second! It could go around the Earth 15 times in one second.

● The strength of electricity is measured in volts. In UK houses it is 240 volts, in the USA it is 115 volts. The wires from a power station carry more than 500,000 volts.

Towers called pylons hold the wires far away from the ground, so people and animals below are safe.

MAKE STATIC ELECTRICITY

Static electricity is electricity which stays still. To make some static electricity, rub a balloon on a woollen jumper. Then see how it makes the balloon stick to a wall.

The electricity comes into each house through a meter box, which counts how much electricity is used.

At a substation, another transformer makes the electricity less strong, so that it is ready to be used in houses.

The electricity flows from the substation to the houses through underground cables or overhead wires.

How do light bulbs shine?

Light bulbs shine because the very thin wire inside, the filament, gets extremely hot. When you turn on a switch the electricity flows along a wire and into the light bulb. The electricity has to force its way through the filament, making it so hot that it glows, giving out light.

MAKE A CIRCUIT

To make a circuit, electricity has to flow in a circle.

1 Attach two pieces of wire to a small block of wood with two drawing pins.

2 Join the end of one wire to a battery and join the other wire to a bulb and then to the battery.

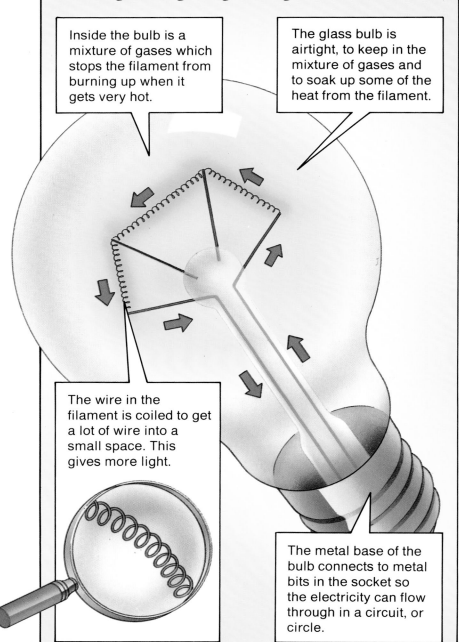

Inside the bulb is a mixture of gases which stops the filament from burning up when it gets very hot.

The glass bulb is airtight, to keep in the mixture of gases and to soak up some of the heat from the filament.

The wire in the filament is coiled to get a lot of wire into a small space. This gives more light.

The metal base of the bulb connects to metal bits in the socket so the electricity can flow through in a circuit, or circle.

ON   OFF

3 Open a paper clip and hook one end under one of the drawing pins.

4 When the paper clip touches both pins it makes a circuit and switches the bulb on. Switch the bulb off by moving the paper clip away from one pin.

Why do some lights flicker?

Some lights flicker when they are first switched on because the special gas inside them is too cold for the electric current to flow through it properly. When the gas heats up, the light becomes a steady glow. These are called fluorescent lights.

The inside of the tube is coated with a chemical that glows when it's hit by the particles – this gives us light.

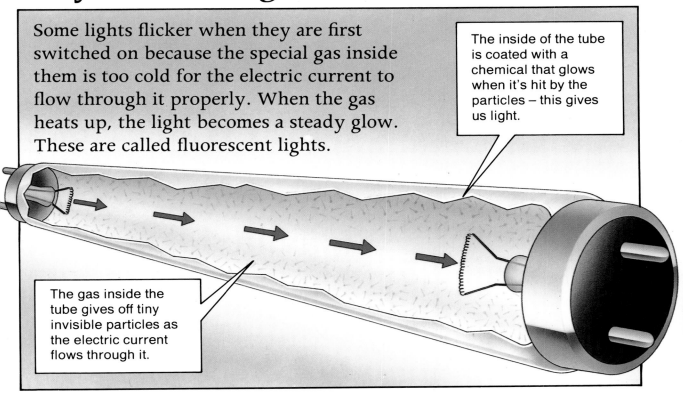

The gas inside the tube gives off tiny invisible particles as the electric current flows through it.

How does a torch work?

A torch has batteries inside it. These supply the electricity to light the bulb. When a torch is switched on, a circuit is made between the batteries and the bulb.

The switch slides along to make contact and complete the circuit, or pushes back to break the circuit and turn off the bulb.

OFF

ON

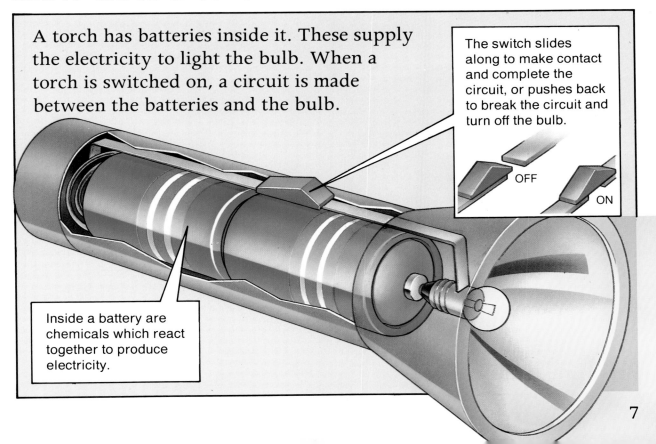

Inside a battery are chemicals which react together to produce electricity.

How does a cooker work?

An electric cooker turns electricity into heat. The electricity pushes its way through a special wire called an element, which becomes very hot. Each element is held inside a metal ring either on top of or inside the oven. As the element heats up, the heat passes through the ring to cook the food.

COOKING FACTS

● Some new cookers cook with light. Instead of an element, they have a powerful lamp that shines light and heat up from below. This is the same type of lamp as in a strong car headlight!

● The first proper cookbook, *Hedypathia*, was written by the Ancient Greek Archestratus 2400 years ago.

Inside each ring there is a special powder which lets the heat through to the ring but stops the electric current.

Powder

Element

A control knob changes the amount of electricity going to each element, to make it warmer or cooler.

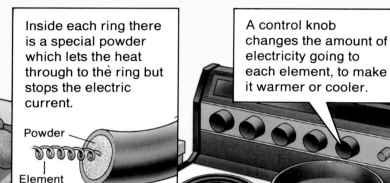

Some rings have a thermostat, a switch which turns off when too hot and on when too cool. As the switch heats up it bends away to break the circuit. As it cools it straightens and makes the circuit again.

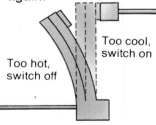

Too cool, switch on

Too hot, switch off

The oven door and sides contain an insulating material which stops most of the heat escaping from the oven.

An electric fan blows the hot air around the oven. This helps to spread the heat, so that the food cooks evenly.

How does a microwave oven work?

Microwaves are invisible waves of energy, like radio waves. When they are beamed strongly into food, they make the watery parts vibrate, or shake, and become hot. This heat is passed through the food and gradually cooks it from within.

The magnetron is the part of a microwave oven that makes the microwaves.

The microwaves are beamed at a metal fan which scatters them around the oven.

Beams of microwaves

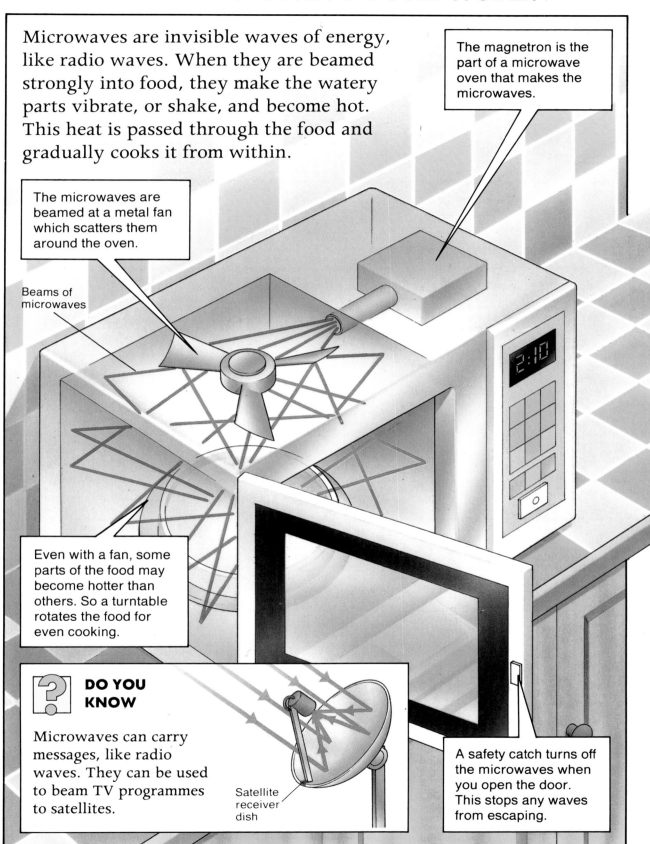

Even with a fan, some parts of the food may become hotter than others. So a turntable rotates the food for even cooking.

? DO YOU KNOW

Microwaves can carry messages, like radio waves. They can be used to beam TV programmes to satellites.

Satellite receiver dish

A safety catch turns off the microwaves when you open the door. This stops any waves from escaping.

How does a flask keep drinks hot?

A vacuum flask keeps drinks hot by stopping the movement of heat out of the flask. There is a gap between the flask's outer case and the inner container. This gap has nothing in it, not even air – it is a vacuum. Heat cannot move very easily across a vacuum, so it is not lost through the sides of the flask. And a tight-fitting stopper prevents heat from leaking out of the top of the flask.

VACUUM FACTS

● The first vacuum flask was invented by the Scottish scientist James Dewar in 1892. The flask was used to keep oxygen in liquid form at very cold temperatures – well below zero!

● Space is almost a vacuum, but there are some things floating in it, like specks of dust and particles of gas.

The stopper is usually made of thick plastic or cork. These materials are good insulators since they keep the heat in.

Air in the gap would carry heat from the container to the case to be lost. The vacuum stops this happening.

The inside walls are shiny to reflect, or send back, heat waves from the contents.

Flasks can also keep heat out, so they can be used for keeping things cold.

 DO YOU KNOW

In 1973, a panel on the US Skylab space station came off in space. The astronauts got too hot in the Sun's glare. So they fixed up a shiny shield to reflect the heat, like the shiny lining in a vacuum flask.

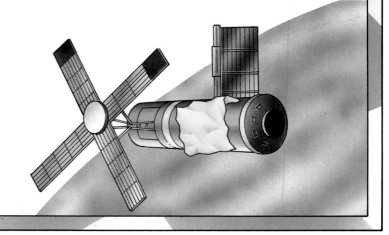

How does a refrigerator keep food cold?

A refrigerator keeps food cold by moving heat from inside to outside. A liquid flows around a circuit of pipes. As it flows it changes from a liquid to a gas and takes up heat from inside the fridge. The pipes carry the gas outside the fridge to give off heat.

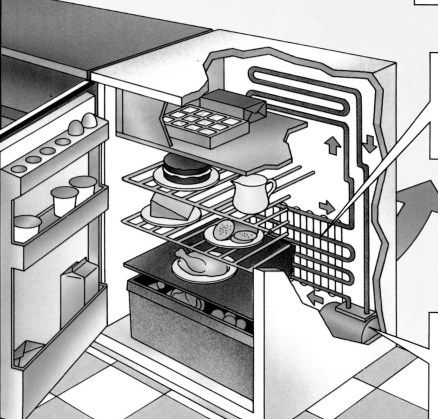

The liquid in the pipes inside the fridge changes into a gas. As it does so, it takes up heat from the food and air, making them cold.

Pipes carry the gas behind the fridge, where it gives off heat to the surrounding air.

The pipes then take the gas through a part of the fridge called a compressor. Here, it is turned back into a liquid.

 MAKE YOUR OWN REFRIGERATOR

When a liquid turns into a gas, taking up heat as it does so, this is called evaporation. Fridges keep food cold by evaporation.

1 Stand a clay flower-pot in a bowl of water.

2 As the water turns to water vapour (a gas) and evaporates from the flower pot, it will draw heat away from anything underneath it.

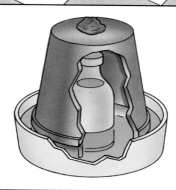

What is a telecommunications network?

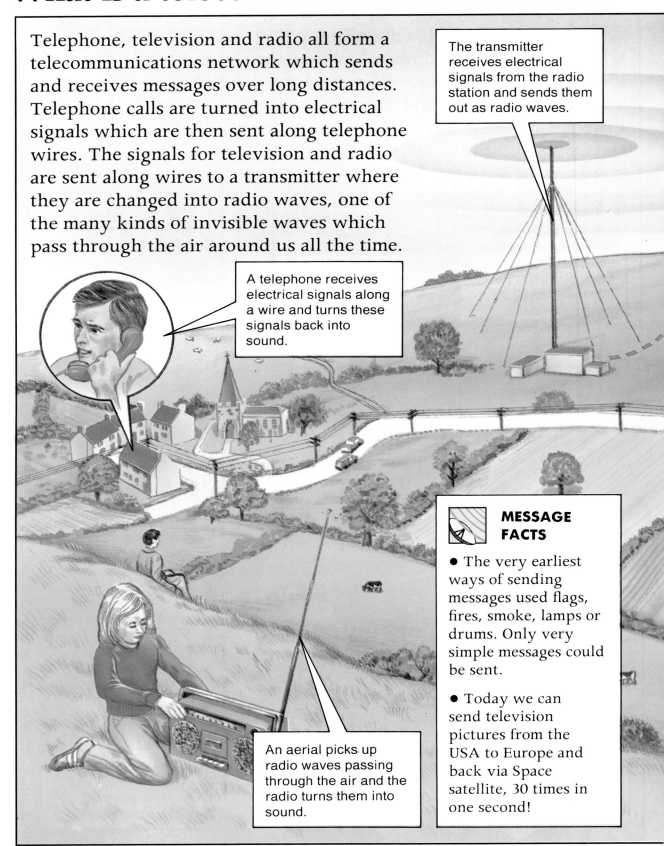

Telephone, television and radio all form a telecommunications network which sends and receives messages over long distances. Telephone calls are turned into electrical signals which are then sent along telephone wires. The signals for television and radio are sent along wires to a transmitter where they are changed into radio waves, one of the many kinds of invisible waves which pass through the air around us all the time.

The transmitter receives electrical signals from the radio station and sends them out as radio waves.

A telephone receives electrical signals along a wire and turns these signals back into sound.

An aerial picks up radio waves passing through the air and the radio turns them into sound.

MESSAGE FACTS

● The very earliest ways of sending messages used flags, fires, smoke, lamps or drums. Only very simple messages could be sent.

● Today we can send television pictures from the USA to Europe and back via Space satellite, 30 times in one second!

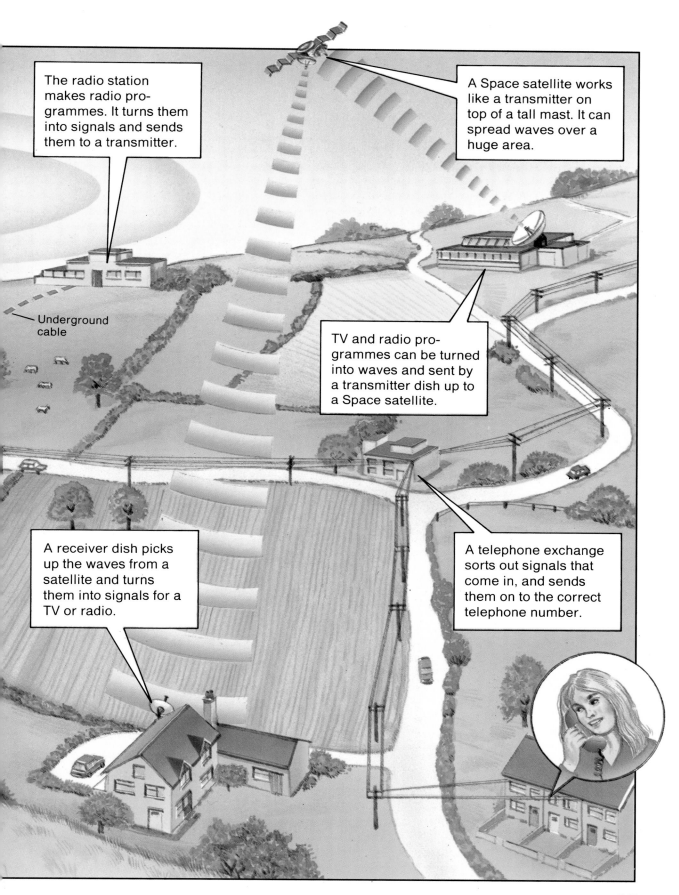

The radio station makes radio pro-grammes. It turns them into signals and sends them to a transmitter.

A Space satellite works like a transmitter on top of a tall mast. It can spread waves over a huge area.

Underground cable

TV and radio pro-grammes can be turned into waves and sent by a transmitter dish up to a Space satellite.

A receiver dish picks up the waves from a satellite and turns them into signals for a TV or radio.

A telephone exchange sorts out signals that come in, and sends them on to the correct telephone number.

How does a radio work?

A radio detects, or picks up, radio waves with its aerial, and turns these into tiny electrical signals with its tuner. It then makes the signals stronger in its amplifier, and turns them into sound waves with its speakers. Radios run on electrical power, either from batteries inside the case, or from a plug and socket.

DO YOU KNOW

Some modern radios tune themselves. You press a tuning button and the tuner searches electronically for the next radio station along the scale whose signals are strong enough to be received clearly. It then automatically locks on to those signals.

A volume knob alters the power of the amplifer, which controls the loudness of the sound waves.

A tuning knob selects which station's waves the radio receives. It moves a pointer along a tuning scale.

Aerial

The amplifier boosts the weak signals it receives from the tuner, so that they are strong enough to work the speakers.

Speaker

Electrical signals at the back of the speaker make its front part shake, or vibrate, producing sounds.

RADIO FACTS

• The Golden Age of radio was from about 1925 to 1955. Television then began to take over.

• The first radio broadcast was to ships in the Atlantic Ocean by Professor Reginald Fessenden, in 1906. The transmitter was an aerial 128 metres high.

• The first radio station to broadcast regular programmes was KDKA in Pittsburg, USA. It began sending out music and sports programmes in 1920.

How does a telephone work?

A telephone changes the sound of your voice into electrical signals and sends them along wires to the telephone exchange. From here, the signals are sent to the telephone of the person you are talking to, where they are changed back into sounds. Signals also travel from the other person's telephone to yours, so you can hear their voice.

 DO YOU KNOW

Alexander Graham Bell invented the telephone in 1876, and spoke the first words into it. He called his assistant saying, 'Mr Watson, come here, I want you.'

A switch in the base of the telephone turns it off when you put the receiver down. Or you press the switch to make another call.

A small loudspeaker in the receiver's earpiece turns signals into sound waves, which your ear picks up.

A loudspeaker in the base makes a chirping or ringing noise, which means that someone is telephoning you.

A microphone in the mouthpiece turns your voice's sound waves. into electrical signals. These travel into the telephone base.

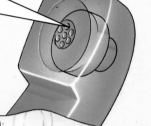

 MAKE A TELEPHONE

1 Find two empty, clean yogurt cartons and make a small hole in the base of each one.

2 Thread the end of a long piece of string through each hole, and tie it in a knot. With a friend, pull the pots

apart so that the string stretches fairly tight.

3 Speak into your pot while your friend holds the other pot to his or her ear. Your pot turns your voice's sound waves into vibrations. These travel along the string and are turned back into sound by the other pot.

How does a television work?

A television set changes electrical signals into pictures on the screen and sounds from the loudspeaker. The television aerial detects waves sent from the transmitter. These waves are turned into signals by the television's tuner. The signals are made more powerful by electronic circuits. Then they are turned into streams of invisible particles called electrons, which are fired by electron guns on to the back of the screen. Where the electrons hit the screen they make it glow, forming a picture.

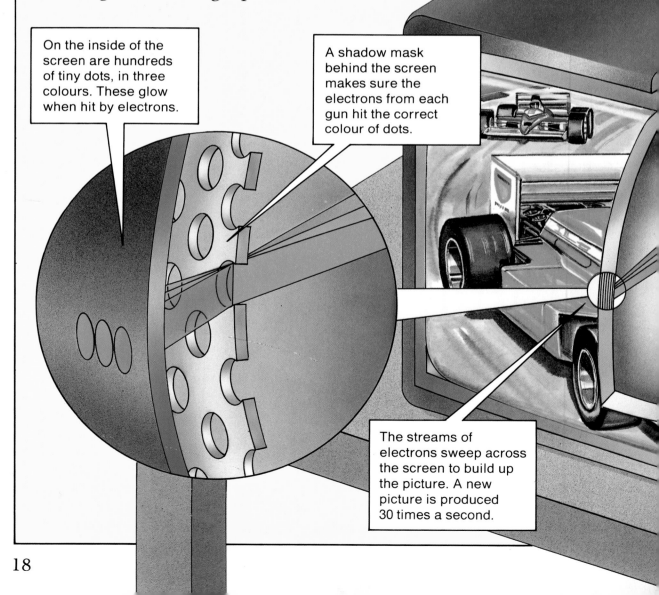

On the inside of the screen are hundreds of tiny dots, in three colours. These glow when hit by electrons.

A shadow mask behind the screen makes sure the electrons from each gun hit the correct colour of dots.

The streams of electrons sweep across the screen to build up the picture. A new picture is produced 30 times a second.

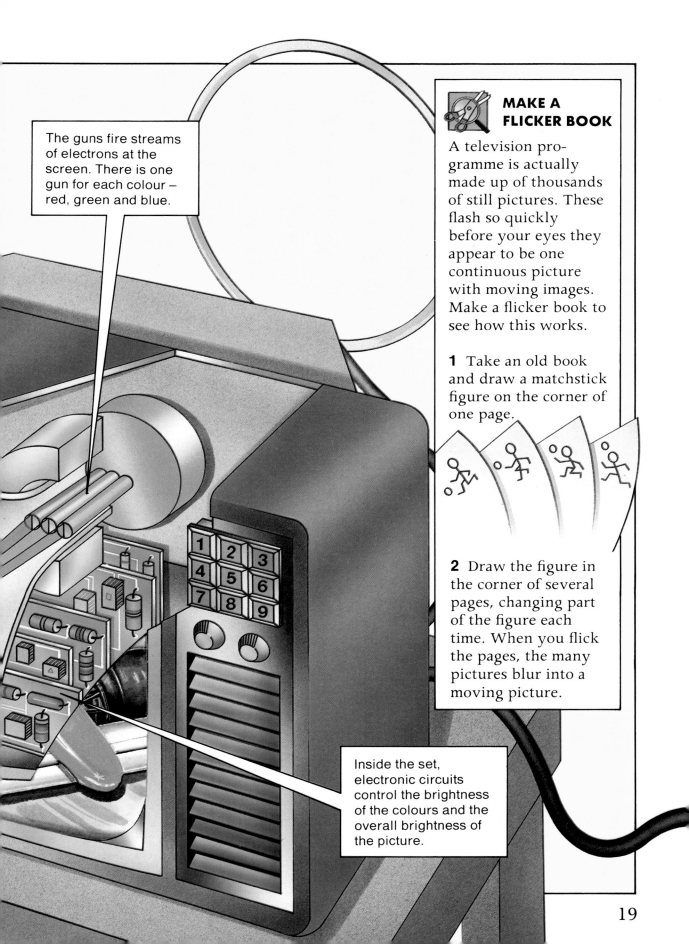

The guns fire streams of electrons at the screen. There is one gun for each colour – red, green and blue.

MAKE A FLICKER BOOK

A television pro-gramme is actually made up of thousands of still pictures. These flash so quickly before your eyes they appear to be one continuous picture with moving images. Make a flicker book to see how this works.

1 Take an old book and draw a matchstick figure on the corner of one page.

2 Draw the figure in the corner of several pages, changing part of the figure each time. When you flick the pages, the many pictures blur into a moving picture.

Inside the set, electronic circuits control the brightness of the colours and the overall brightness of the picture.

How do cassette players work?

Cassette players work by moving a tape past a tape head. A cassette tape contains patches of magnetism, which are codes for the sounds recorded on it. The tape head changes these magnetic codes into electrical signals. These are made more powerful by an amplifier and then sent to a loudspeaker, which turns the signals into sounds.

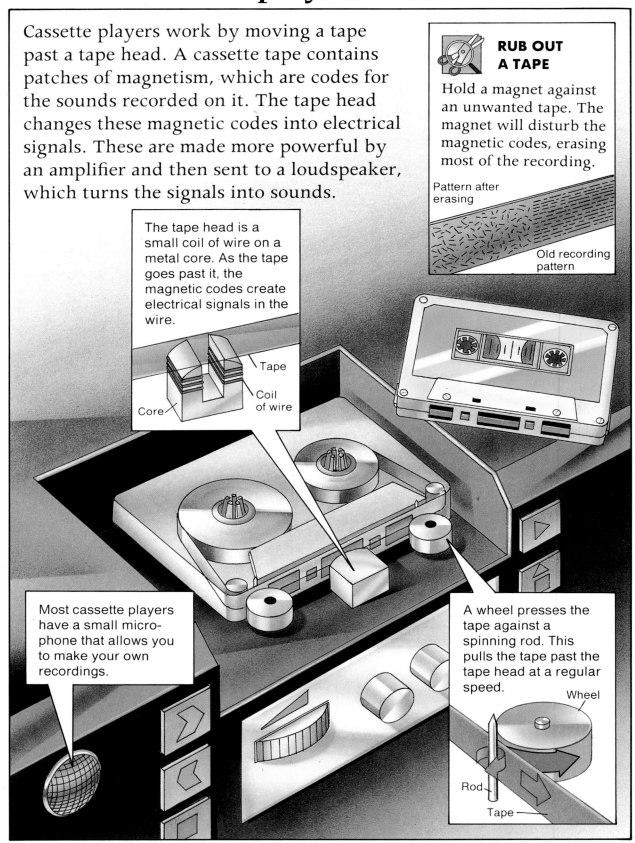

RUB OUT A TAPE

Hold a magnet against an unwanted tape. The magnet will disturb the magnetic codes, erasing most of the recording.

Pattern after erasing

Old recording pattern

The tape head is a small coil of wire on a metal core. As the tape goes past it, the magnetic codes create electrical signals in the wire.

Tape

Coil of wire

Core

Most cassette players have a small microphone that allows you to make your own recordings.

A wheel presses the tape against a spinning rod. This pulls the tape past the tape head at a regular speed.

Wheel

Rod

Tape

How do video recorders work?

Like the cassette player opposite, a video recorder uses a tape head to read or record magnetic codes on a tape. But these codes contain pictures as well as sounds.

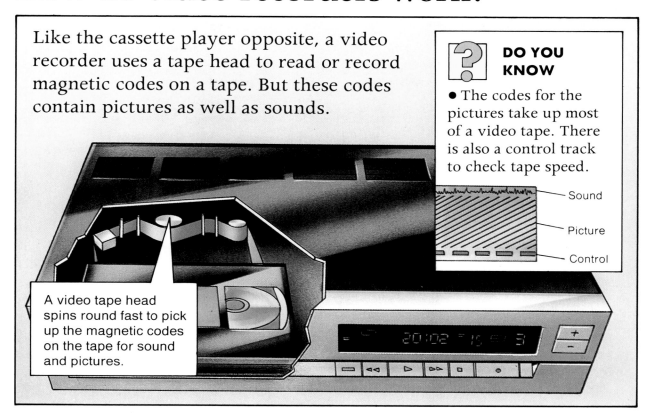

A video tape head spins round fast to pick up the magnetic codes on the tape for sound and pictures.

DO YOU KNOW

● The codes for the pictures take up most of a video tape. There is also a control track to check tape speed.

- Sound
- Picture
- Control

How do calculators work?

A calculator is a simple type of computer. It calculates, or does sums, by treating numbers as electrical signals, using the tiny electrical circuits in a microchip.

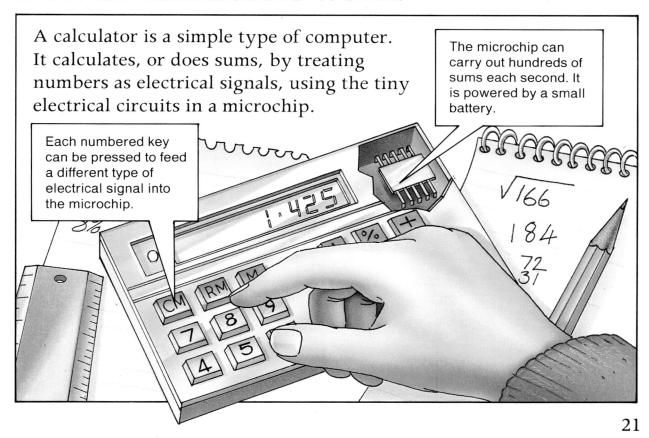

The microchip can carry out hundreds of sums each second. It is powered by a small battery.

Each numbered key can be pressed to feed a different type of electrical signal into the microchip.

$\sqrt{166}$

184

72
31

What do computers do?

Computers turn all sorts of information into electrical signals in order to work with the information. Information can be fed into and out of a computer using machines called input and output units. A computer can do many different things with this information by following a list of instructions. This list is called a program and it is stored inside the computer.

 DO YOU KNOW

Computers can do many very different jobs. They are used, for example, to fly aircraft and to forecast the weather, to control satellites in Space and to design cars.

 COMPUTER FACTS

● The heart of a computer is a Central Processing Unit (CPU). This is where the signals from an input unit are altered according to the program and sent to an output unit.

● A computer has its own memory. Any information in this memory is lost when the computer is switched off, so information is stored on discs or tapes.

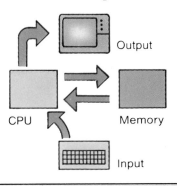

Output

CPU

Memory

Input

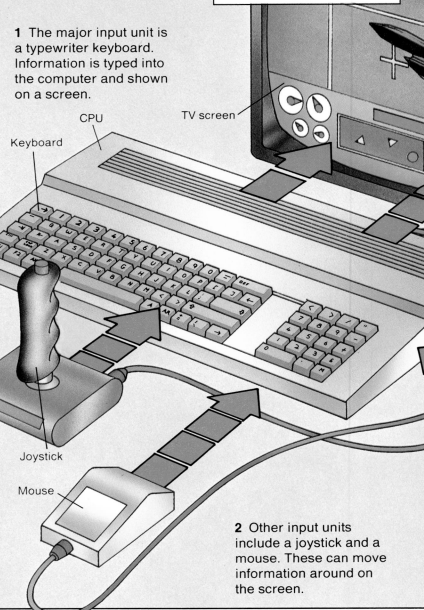

1 The major input unit is a typewriter keyboard. Information is typed into the computer and shown on a screen.

CPU

Keyboard

TV screen

Joystick

Mouse

2 Other input units include a joystick and a mouse. These can move information around on the screen.

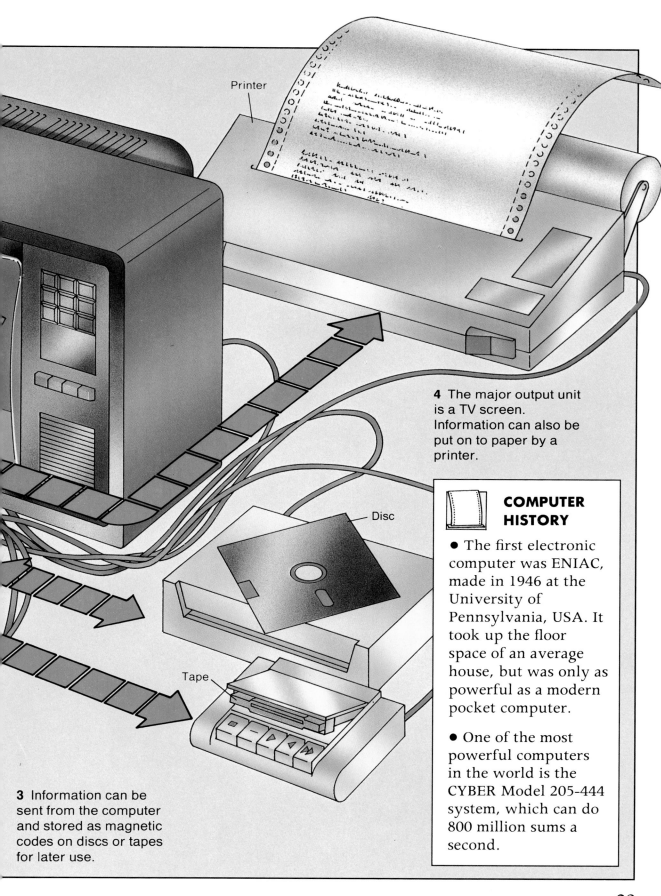

Printer

4 The major output unit is a TV screen. Information can also be put on to paper by a printer.

Disc

Tape

3 Information can be sent from the computer and stored as magnetic codes on discs or tapes for later use.

COMPUTER HISTORY

● The first electronic computer was ENIAC, made in 1946 at the University of Pennsylvania, USA. It took up the floor space of an average house, but was only as powerful as a modern pocket computer.

● One of the most powerful computers in the world is the CYBER Model 205-444 system, which can do 800 million sums a second.

How does a camera take photos?

To take a photo, a camera lets in light from a scene or an image in front of it and directs the light on to a piece of photographic film. The light affects the chemicals that coat the film and makes a picture on it. When the film is developed it is bathed in chemicals which make this picture permanent. The picture can then be printed on to photographic paper.

A shutter button opens the shutter for a fraction of a second, to let the right amount of light into the camera.

 MAKE A CAMERA

This simple pinhole camera shows how a real camera works.

1 Cut one side out of an empty cardboard box. Paint the inside black.

2 Tape a piece of thin tracing paper over the missing side.

3 Make a tiny pinhole in the middle of the side opposite.

4 Set up the camera in a room with the pinhole side facing a bright window. Put an object in front of the window and cover up any other sources of light.

5 The pinhole is the lens. It directs the light on to the tracing paper, which is the film. You should see an upside-down picture of the window on the film. A real camera lens also turns the picture upside-down.

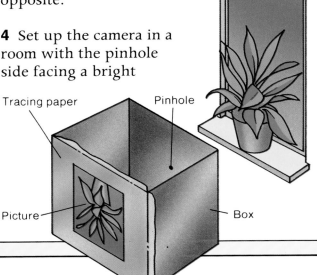

Tracing paper

Pinhole

Picture

Box

Photographic film is a long roll of plastic with a chemical coating. It winds along for each new photograph.

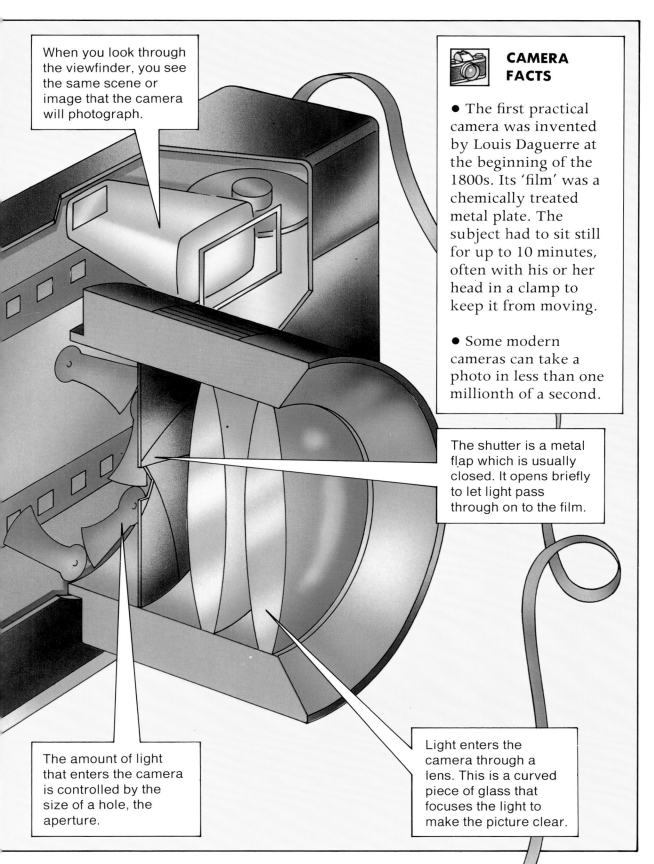

When you look through the viewfinder, you see the same scene or image that the camera will photograph.

CAMERA FACTS

● The first practical camera was invented by Louis Daguerre at the beginning of the 1800s. Its 'film' was a chemically treated metal plate. The subject had to sit still for up to 10 minutes, often with his or her head in a clamp to keep it from moving.

● Some modern cameras can take a photo in less than one millionth of a second.

The shutter is a metal flap which is usually closed. It opens briefly to let light pass through on to the film.

The amount of light that enters the camera is controlled by the size of a hole, the aperture.

Light enters the camera through a lens. This is a curved piece of glass that focuses the light to make the picture clear.

25

Why do some doors open by themselves?

A door that opens automatically, or by itself, does so because an electronic sensor tells it when someone is nearby. The sensor can be a light beam or a pressure mat.

A light beam shines from a sender to a receiver. When the beam is blocked, the receiver tells the doors to open. Alternatively, a pressure mat contains a switch. When you stand on it, your weight closes the switch and makes the doors open.

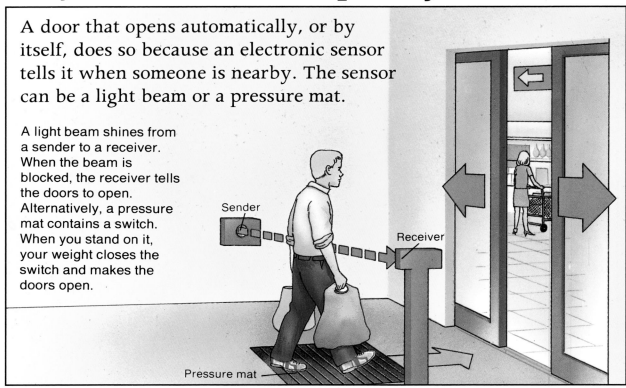

Sender

Receiver

Pressure mat

What are bar codes?

A bar code contains information in the form of black bars of different thicknesses. A machine called a light-reader can turn this code into electronic signals.

A bar code contains information about the object it is printed on, such as its price and identification number.

The light-reader sends the information to a computerized till, which shows it on the display.

How do locks work?

To lock a door, a bolt moves out of the lock and slots into the door frame. Unlocking the door slides this bolt back. The key turns a cylinder which moves the bolt in or out.

When the door is locked, small springs push a row of pins into the metal cylinder so it cannot be turned.

The notches on the key push the pins free of the cylinder so the key can turn the cylinder and move the bolt.

DO YOU KNOW

The Yale lock was invented in 1865, but it works in the same way as the locks used in Ancient Egypt.

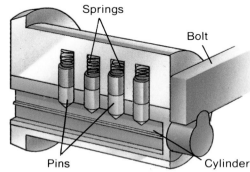

Springs

Bolt

Pins

Cylinder

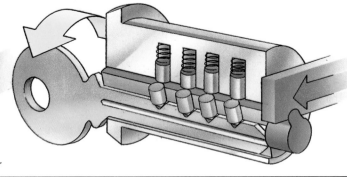

How do doorbells work?

A doorbell uses electricity to make a hammer strike a bell. When you press the bell button a magnet is turned on and this pulls the metal hammer against the bell.

The bell button is part of a circuit. Pressing it allows electricity to flow around the circuit to the magnet.

The magnet switches on and off many times, making the hammer strike the bell until the button is released.

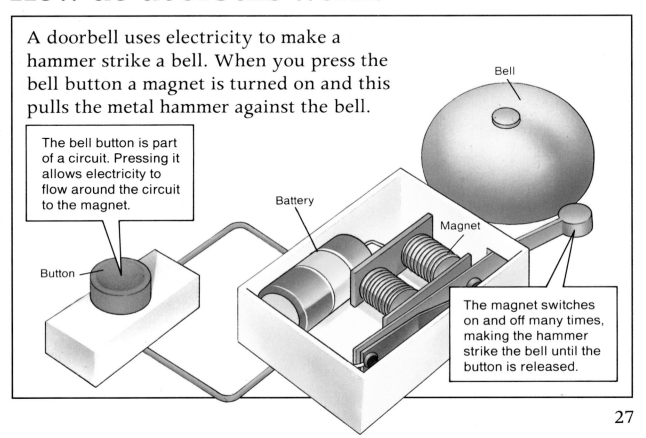

Bell

Battery

Magnet

Button

How do clocks work?

Inside a clock, a wound-up spring slowly unwinds and turns a notched wheel. This wheel drives a series of other wheels which make the hands move around the clock-face.

● A digital watch has no springs or wheels. It is powered by a small battery which makes a tiny crystal vibrate, or shake. This produces a stream of electrical signals. A microchip counts the signals and shows the time as changing numbers.

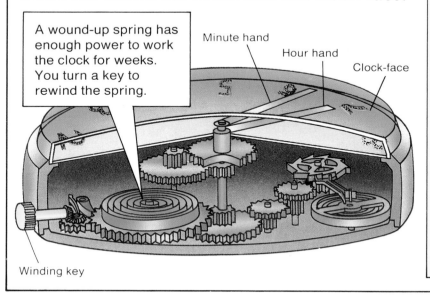

A wound-up spring has enough power to work the clock for weeks. You turn a key to rewind the spring.

Minute hand

Hour hand

Clock-face

Winding key

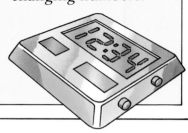

How do scales work?

When something is put into a scale's pan it presses down on a long bar. This pulls down a spring which makes a pointer move around the scale's numbered face.

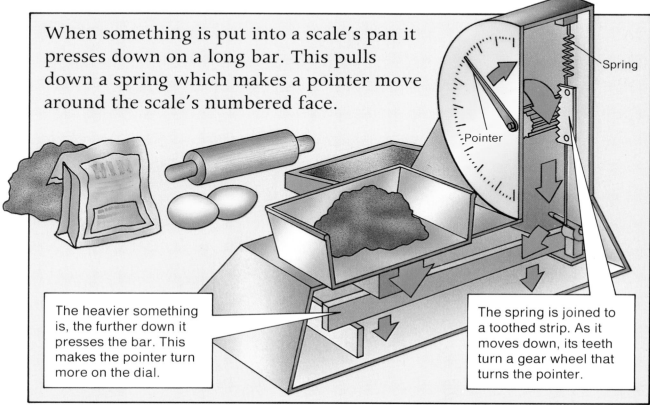

Spring

Pointer

The heavier something is, the further down it presses the bar. This makes the pointer turn more on the dial.

The spring is joined to a toothed strip. As it moves down, its teeth turn a gear wheel that turns the pointer.

28

How do screwdrivers work?

A screwdriver is a kind of lever which goes in a circle. When you turn the handle, the force of the turn travels down the shaft to the blade and then to the screw.

At the top of the screwdriver the hand moves through a large circle in order to turn the screwdriver.

At the bottom of the screwdriver the distance to turn is smaller, so there is greater force here to turn the screw.

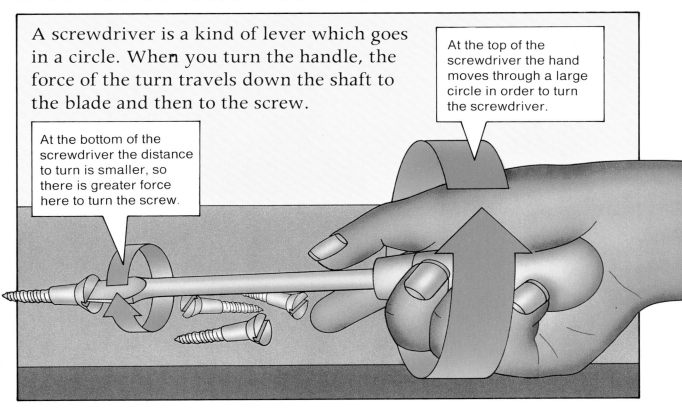

How do can openers work?

A can opener is a kind of double-lever. You squeeze the handles a long way with a small force. This moves the blade a short distance, but with great force.

The handles must be squeezed together, or the force on the blade will weaken and the lid will push it out.

Turnkey

Once the wedge-shaped blade is pushed into the can, a turnkey is turned to move the blade along.

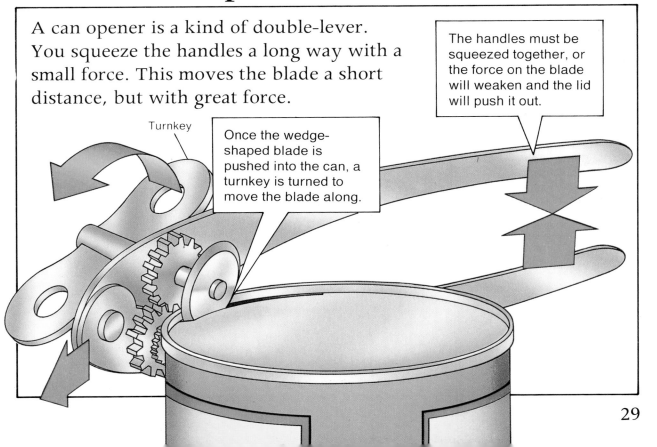

How do zips work?

As a zip is done up, the sliding part presses together two rows of tiny teeth and makes them lock together. To undo a zip, this slide forces the rows of teeth apart.

In the centre of the slide there is a wedge. This separates the two rows of teeth when the slide is pulled down.

There is a small space under each tooth. As the teeth are forced together, each one slots into the space under the tooth above.

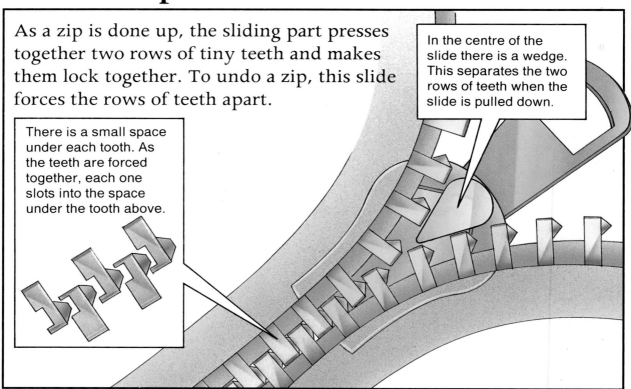

How do bicycle gears work?

Bicycle gears control the number of times the back wheel is turned round for each turn of the pedals. The chain is moved to a different-sized cog wheel for each gear.

High gears are for going downhill. You pedal more slowly to produce a fast turn of the back wheel.

Low gears are for going uphill. You pedal faster to produce a slow, strong turn of the back wheel.

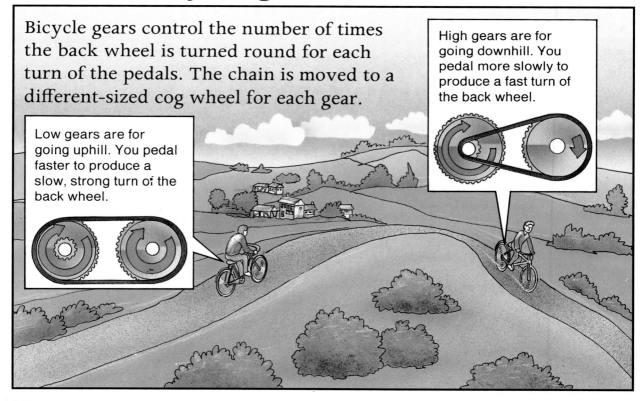

How do bicycle pumps work?

A bicycle pump pulls in air and pushes it through a connecting tube into a bicycle tyre. A valve inside the pump controls the flow of air.

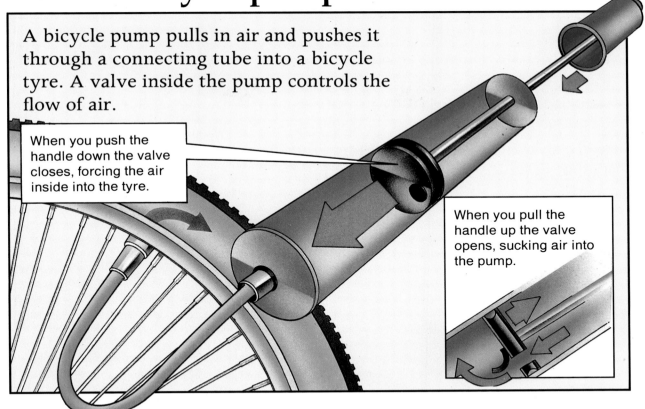

When you push the handle down the valve closes, forcing the air inside into the tyre.

When you pull the handle up the valve opens, sucking air into the pump.

How do aerosol sprays work?

Inside an aerosol can, a gas is packed so tightly it forces a liquid up a tube to a nozzle. When the button is pressed, the nozzle opens and the contents spray out.

A valve in the nozzle opens to let the gas and liquid out. The small hole breaks the liquid into a fine spray.

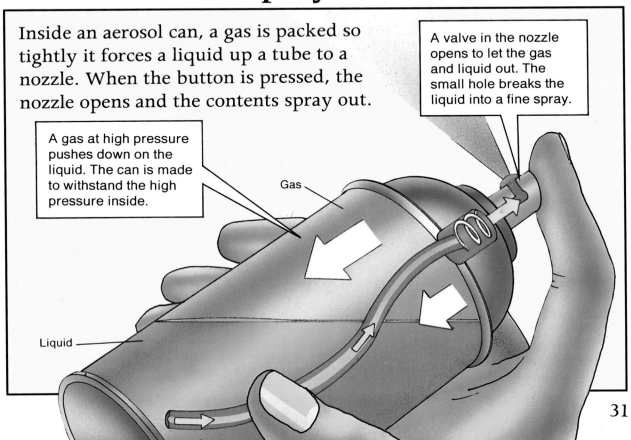

A gas at high pressure pushes down on the liquid. The can is made to withstand the high pressure inside.

Gas

Liquid

How do car engines work?

Car engines burn petrol to create the power that makes the car move. When a car is driven, hundreds of small explosions happen in the engine every minute as the petrol is burned. The explosions occur inside cylinders. In each cylinder, the force of each explosion pushes down a piston. The pistons are connected to a crankshaft. Their movement turns the crankshaft round and this power is carried to the car's gearbox.

DO YOU KNOW

Engine power is usually measured in horsepower. This was originally the pulling power of a good farm horse!

An average family car produces about 50–80 horsepower. A Grand Prix racing car produces more than 500 horsepower.

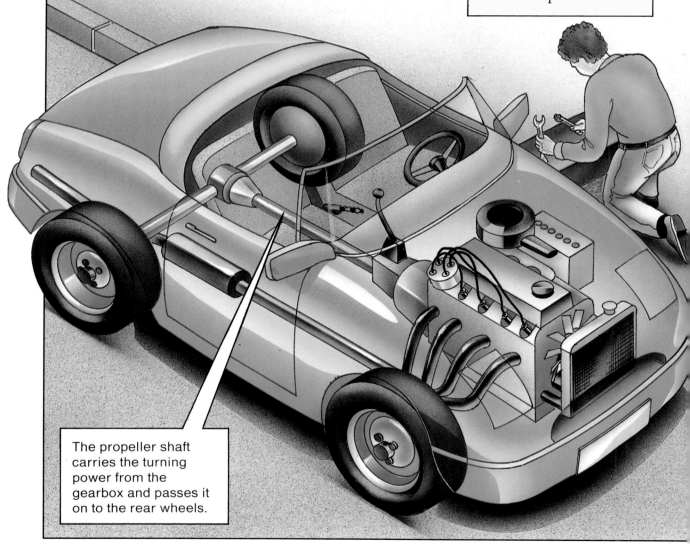

The propeller shaft carries the turning power from the gearbox and passes it on to the rear wheels.

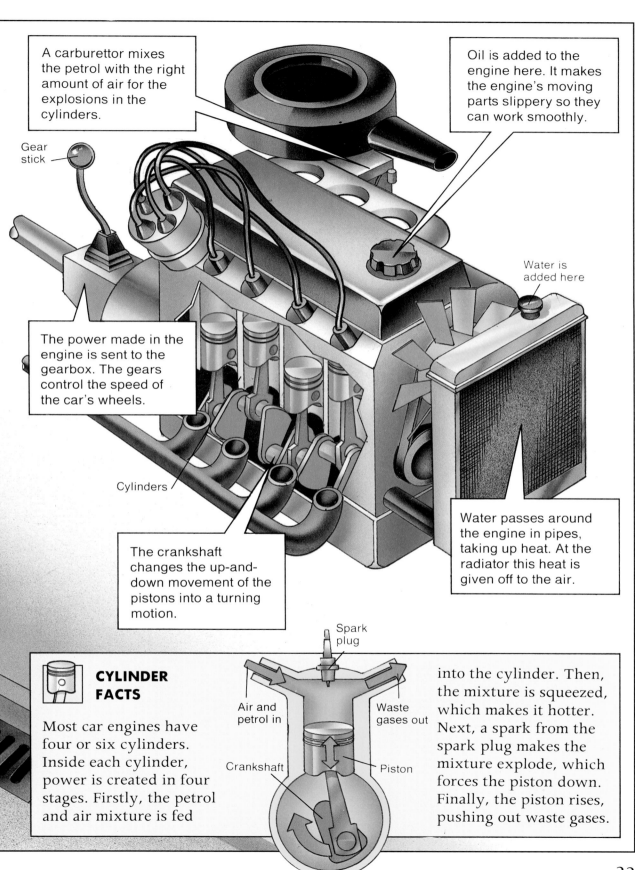

A carburettor mixes the petrol with the right amount of air for the explosions in the cylinders.

Oil is added to the engine here. It makes the engine's moving parts slippery so they can work smoothly.

Gear stick

Water is added here

The power made in the engine is sent to the gearbox. The gears control the speed of the car's wheels.

Cylinders

The crankshaft changes the up-and-down movement of the pistons into a turning motion.

Water passes around the engine in pipes, taking up heat. At the radiator this heat is given off to the air.

Spark plug

CYLINDER FACTS

Air and petrol in

Waste gases out

Crankshaft

Piston

Most car engines have four or six cylinders. Inside each cylinder, power is created in four stages. Firstly, the petrol and air mixture is fed into the cylinder. Then, the mixture is squeezed, which makes it hotter. Next, a spark from the spark plug makes the mixture explode, which forces the piston down. Finally, the piston rises, pushing out waste gases.

Where does tap water come from?

Tap water comes from rain which falls into a storage reservoir, or trickles through the soil into a river. It is then drawn off in pipes and treated to make it clean and safe to drink. It is pumped to each house along a large pipe under the ground, called a water main. Water from the main flows up into each house's roof-space, where it fills up a cold water tank. Usually, the kitchen cold tap is connected directly to the main.

The cold water tank sends water to all the cold taps in the house. It also sends water to the hot water tank.

DO YOU KNOW

In countries such as the UK and the USA, each person uses up to 300 litres of water a day. This includes water for drinking and cooking, water for the bath (80 litres), water for washing clothes and bedding, and water for flushing the lavatory (20 litres). In some countries, each person uses only 25 litres a day.

The water main carries water at high pressure from a larger main, usually buried under a nearby road or path.

Hot water tank

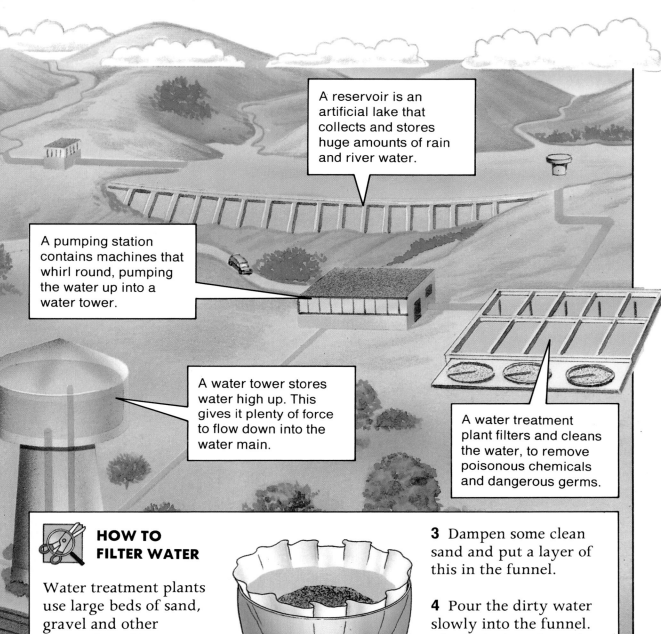

A reservoir is an artificial lake that collects and stores huge amounts of rain and river water.

A pumping station contains machines that whirl round, pumping the water up into a water tower.

A water tower stores water high up. This gives it plenty of force to flow down into the water main.

A water treatment plant filters and cleans the water, to remove poisonous chemicals and dangerous germs.

HOW TO FILTER WATER

Water treatment plants use large beds of sand, gravel and other materials to filter water. You can do the same thing on a smaller scale.

1 Mix some soil or mud in water, to make it dirty.

2 Place a funnel, or the cut-off top of a plastic bottle, in a glass jar. Put a cone-shaped coffee filter in the funnel.

3 Dampen some clean sand and put a layer of this in the funnel.

4 Pour the dirty water slowly into the funnel. The bed of sand traps larger dirt particles, and the filter paper traps smaller ones.

5 The water that drips into the glass jar should look cleaner.

Warning – don't drink any of this water – it may still contain some harmful germs.

What happens when you turn on a tap?

As you turn on a water tap, you open a gap which allows the water in the pipe to come out. The water is always trying to push its way out, but it is stopped by a small piece of rubber called a washer which blocks the top of the pipe. When you turn on the tap, a screw lifts away from the washer. The water pushes the washer up and flows past.

MAKE A WASHER

You can see how a tap works by making your own washer from modelling clay.

1 Put a blob of clay on to the end of a pencil. Fasten a piece of clear polythene over it with an elastic band.

2 Press the clay washer into the neck of a cut-off plastic bottle. Hold the bottle upside down and fill it with water.

3 Lift the washer to let water flow. Press it down to close your tap.

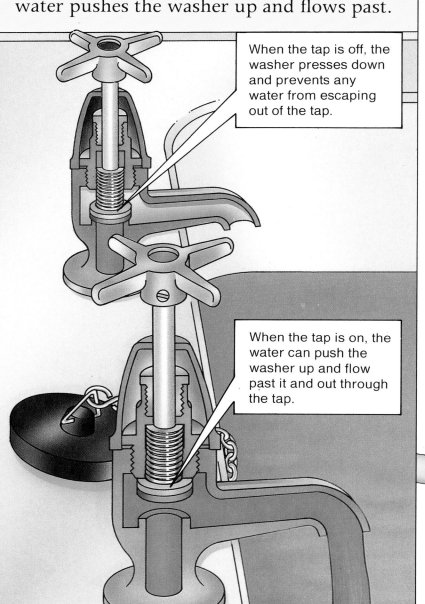

When the tap is off, the washer presses down and prevents any water from escaping out of the tap.

When the tap is on, the water can push the washer up and flow past it and out through the tap.

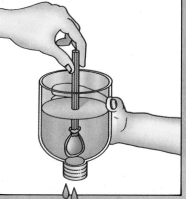

How do lavatories flush?

Lavatories flush by sending new water into the bowl to push out the dirty water. Inside a cistern there is a compartment called a bell. When you press the handle, water inside the bell goes into the bowl, sucking other water in the cistern with it.

The handle works a lever which raises a disc in the bell. The disc pushes some water up, and into the bowl.

As the cistern refills, the float rises and gradually closes the valve. This stops too much water coming in.

Cistern

Bell

Disc

A float in the cistern goes down as the water level falls. This makes a valve open so the cistern can refill.

Bowl

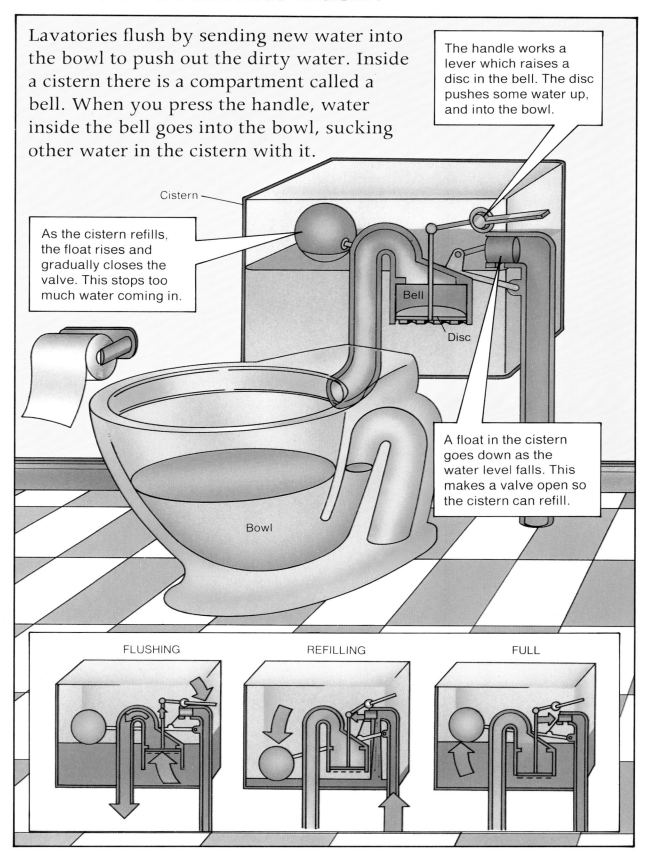

FLUSHING

REFILLING

FULL

What happens to all our rubbish?

For many years, people have mixed up different types of rubbish and thrown them all away, to be buried in enormous pits on land or put in containers sunk into the sea. However, we will gradually run out of places to dump rubbish. We will also run out of the materials that are needed to make new things. Some rubbish is now recycled, or remade, so it can be used again.

DO YOU KNOW

Recycling saves on the fuel that is used to make things. Less heat is needed to recycle glass, paper and tin than to make them from the beginning. So less fuel is used up to produce the heat.

Glass bottles and jars can be collected in bottle banks. They will be melted down to make new bottles.

Paper and card can be pulped and made into paper again. This saves more trees from being cut down for paper.

The tin and aluminium in metal cans can be melted down to make new cans, instead of mining yet more metal.

Leftover bits of fruit and vegetables can be put on a compost heap in the garden. They will rot back into the earth.

Useful words

Circuit A circle around which an electric current flows.

Electron An invisibly small particle, or piece of matter.

Evaporation The process by which a liquid turns into a gas.

Insulator A special material that prevents the passage of heat, sound or electricity. For example, insulators help stop heat loss from ovens and vacuum flasks.

Microchip A tiny electronic device containing many miniature circuits that can process or store electrical signals. Microchips are found in many machines, from calculators and cars to computers and washing machines.

Microphone An instrument that picks up sound waves and turns them into electrical signals that can pass along a wire.

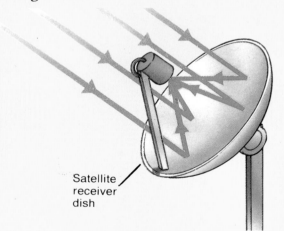

Satellite receiver dish

Microwave A type of invisible wave, similar to radio waves. Microwaves are often used to carry signals to satellites. Inside a microwave oven, microwaves are beamed through food in order to cook it.

Recycle To pass something through a series of treatments which allows it to be reused.

Reservoir A lake that has been built to collect and store water.

Satellite An object circling another object. For example, the Moon is a satellite of the Earth. Artificial satellites are put into Space to be used for telecommunications.

Telecommunications The sending and receiving of information by telephone, telegraph, radio and television.

Thermostat A device that controls temperature automatically. It switches off when too hot and on when too cold.

Transformer A machine that increases or decreases the voltage, or strength, of an electric current.

Vacuum A space that has nothing in it, not even air.

Valve A device that controls the flow of a gas or liquid, usually allowing it to go in one direction only.

Index